W9-CEL-154

U.S. HISTORY TIMELINES

Change and Reform
1814-1860

Jack Zayarny

www.av2books.com

AV² provides enriched content that supplements and complements this book. Weigl's AV² books strive to create inspired learning and engage young minds in a total learning experience.

Your AV² Media Enhanced books come alive with...

Audio
Listen to sections of the book read aloud.

Key Words
Study vocabulary, and complete a matching word activity.

Video
Watch informative video clips.

Quizzes
Test your knowledge.

Go to **www.av2books.com**, and enter this book's unique code.

BOOK CODE

F900627

Embedded Weblinks
Gain additional information for research.

Slide Show
View images and captions, and prepare a presentation.

AV² by Weigl brings you media enhanced books that support active learning.

Try This!
Complete activities and hands-on experiments.

... and much, much more!

Published by AV² by Weigl
350 5th Avenue, 59th Floor
New York, NY 10118
Websites: www.av2books.com   www.weigl.com

Copyright ©2015 AV² by Weigl
All rights reserved. No part of this publication may be reproduced, stored in a retrieval system, or transmitted in any form or by any means, electronic, mechanical, photocopying, recording, or otherwise, without the prior written permission of the publisher.

Library of Congress Control Number: 2014933465

ISBN 978–1–4896–0724–9 (hardcover)
ISBN 978–1–4896–0725–6 (softcover)
ISBN 978–1–4896–0726–3 (single–user eBook)
ISBN 978–1–4896–0727–0 (multi–user eBook)

Printed in the United States of America in North Mankato, Minnesota
1 2 3 4 5 6 7 8 9 0   18 17 16 15 14

052014
WEP301113

Project Coordinator: Aaron Carr
Editor: Pamela Dell
Designer: Mandy Christiansen

Every reasonable effort has been made to trace ownership and to obtain permission to reprint copyright material. The publishers would be pleased to have any errors or omissions brought to their attention so that they may be corrected in subsequent printings.

Weigl acknowledges Getty Images as the primary image supplier for this title.

CONTENTS

2   AV^2 Book Code

4   A Proud Nation

6   The Industrial Revolution

8   Education and Politics

10   Leading the Way

12   Seeing the Light

14   Movement Toward Abolition

16   Reforming Society

18   A Higher Vision

20   Women's Suffrage

22   Nation in Turmoil

24   The Call for Freedom

26   War on the Horizon

28   Activity

30   Brain Teaser

31   Key Words/Index

32   Log on to www.av2books.com

A Proud Nation

Early in the 1800s, a strong sense of pride swept through the new American nation. The United States had fought the British in the War of 1812. Neither side claimed victory, but Great Britain was no longer involved in U.S. affairs. By 1815, Americans were enjoying what some called an "era of good feeling." The people felt their nation had earned a place of power in the world.

With this new strength and positive energy came sweeping change. **Industry** boomed, especially in the North. The South, however, still depended on farming and slave labor.

The fast and sudden growth of the nation strained the government. Americans called for **reform**. **Industrialization** and the growing U.S. population raised questions about **civil rights**, voting rights for women, **abolition**, and other important issues.

THE WAR OF 1812 officially ended with the signing of the Treaty of Ghent on December 24, 1814, in Ghent, Belgium.

1814   1820s   1821–1840   1824–1841   1826–1830s   1831–1863

JAMES MADISON

Fourth U.S. president James Madison had an important role in the creation of the U.S. Constitution. For this, he is known as the Father of the Constitution. He was also one of the Founding Fathers, a group of men who created the U.S. **federal** government. Madison led the United States into the War of 1812.

BATTLE OF NEW ORLEANS, 1815

In December 1814, the Americans and the British agreed to end the War of 1812. This news traveled slowly in the United States, however. One last major battle took place on January 8, 1815. U.S. troops defeated the British at the Battle of New Orleans in Louisiana. That battle was the greatest victory of the entire war for the United States.

NORTH VS. SOUTH

During the reform period, tensions rose between the North and the South. The two regions differed widely on many issues. Northerners were in favor of change. Southerners, however, wanted to keep their way of life.

The North saw the rise of industry as a way to improve the nation's **economy**. The economy of the South was based on farming. Southerners needed slave labor to keep that economy strong and growing.

The Industrial Revolution

The early 1800s saw a **revolution** in industry. By 1820, this Industrial Revolution was undeniable. Machines soon replaced hand labor in many businesses. Factory assembly lines came into use. This system made production quicker and easier, especially in industries such as weaving and mining. Electrical power also sped up production. The Industrial Revolution brought benefits to other industries as well, especially transportation. Steam power greatly improved the railroad.

Factories took hold mainly in the North. Much of the South's money came from growing cotton and turning it into woven fabrics. In both regions, the number of workers grew rapidly.

An interest in another kind of reform arose at this time. Workers began to organize **labor unions** to improve conditions on the job and to protect workers' rights.

FACTORIES SPRUNG UP all over the northeast. In some states, business owners created whole towns to house workers.

| 1814–1815 | 1820s | 1821–1840 | 1824–1841 | 1826–1830s | 1831–1863 |

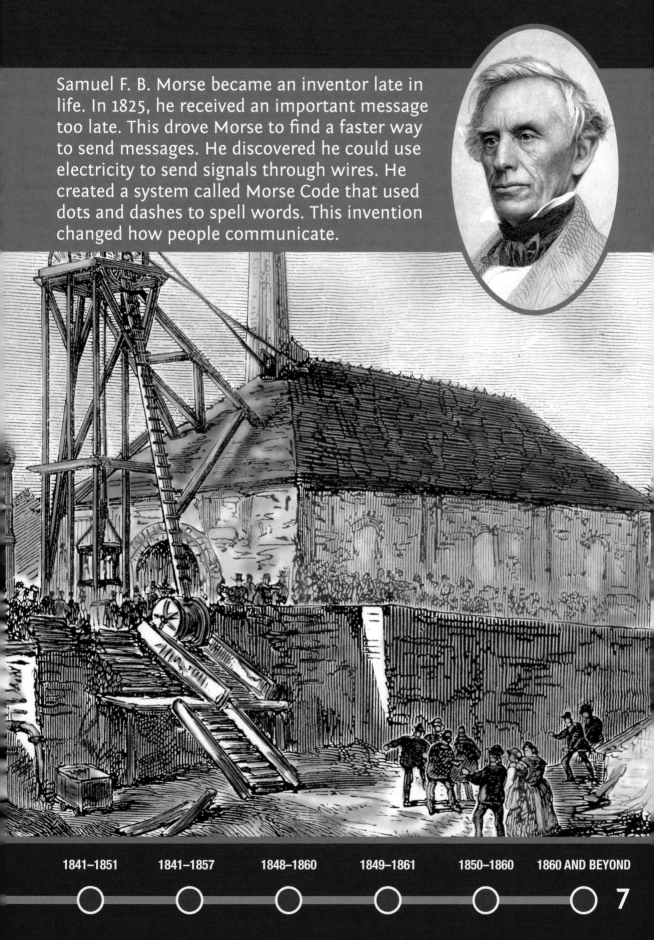

Samuel F. B. Morse became an inventor late in life. In 1825, he received an important message too late. This drove Morse to find a faster way to send messages. He discovered he could use electricity to send signals through wires. He created a system called Morse Code that used dots and dashes to spell words. This invention changed how people communicate.

Education and Politics

In 1821, English High School opened in Boston, Massachusetts. It was the nation's first public high school. English High School was open only to working class boys, but it was a start. At the time, education was mostly a privilege of the rich. By the next decade, this had started to change.

Educational reformers Horace Mann and Henry Barnard were leaders in the Common School movement, which began in 1837. They argued that free education for all would wipe out poverty and crime. Educational reformers felt education could improve the lives of **immigrants** as well.

Political reformers were also hard at work in the early 1800s. With the election of President Andrew Jackson in 1828, **Jacksonian democracy** took hold. At that time, white men who owned land made political decisions. The law kept women, African Americans, and those without land from voting. Reformers brought more equality to the voting process, however. By 1840, 80 percent of those who could vote were going to the **polls**. This was a greater number than ever before.

MCGUFFEY READER

In 1833, Reverend William Holmes McGuffey published a textbook for use in public schools. This book, often called the McGuffey Reader, encouraged students to be honest, kind, and hardworking. It also presented the **ideal** American as white and **Protestant**. The reader offered lessons in history, science, table manners, and other subjects. Many editions were printed in the 1800s. It was the first textbook ever used by millions of Americans.

1814–1815   1820s   1821   1824–1841   1826–1830s   1831–1863

1840

EDUCATIONAL REFORMERS SAW universal education as a way to strengthen the bonds among all classes of people.

Leading the Way

As the nation grew, politics divided many people. By the 1820s, the Democratic-Republican Party was on the rise. In the 1824 presidential election, rival Republicans John Quincy Adams and Andrew Jackson were among the most popular candidates. The party split in two after a fierce disagreement about who had won the election. Supporters of Adams and Jackson eventually formed separate political parties.

During the 1820s and 1830s, the nation's leaders faced more troubles. Many national issues raised heated debate and disagreement among the public. The United States, and its presidents, struggled to deal with change on all fronts.

JOHN QUINCY ADAMS
(IN OFFICE 1825–1829)

John Quincy Adams was the sixth U.S. president and son of second president John Adams. During his one term in office, Adams tried to improve the nation by building a national university and a national bank. He supported the arts and sciences. Adams also proposed a system of railways and canals. This plan was in many ways ahead of its time. However, Adams had little support from either the public or the politicians. Much of what he wanted to accomplish never came to be.

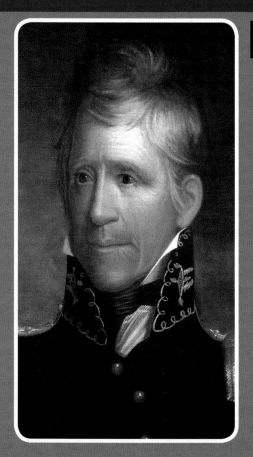

ANDREW JACKSON
(IN OFFICE 1829–1837)

Andrew Jackson was the seventh U.S. president. He is thought to be one of the fathers of the Democratic Party. Jackson wanted to run the government "for the good of the people." During his eight-year presidency, Jackson dealt with two major issues. One was the Nullification Crisis. This disagreement focused on whether states could refuse to uphold federal laws they did not support. Jackson wanted to keep those states from **seceding** from the **Union**. He offered them a **compromise** called the Tariff Act of 1833. This lowered taxes on goods brought into the states.

Jackson's other main challenge was a conflict with the Second Bank of the United States. He felt the bank kept money in the hands of the rich and did not help working-class people. In 1836, Jackson closed the bank and moved its funds into state banks. His control over national spending also allowed him to pay off the national debt.

MARTIN VAN BUREN
(IN OFFICE 1837–1841)

Martin Van Buren was the eighth U.S. president. He faced many problems in his efforts to reform the nation. The Panic of 1837 drove down the nation's economy and hurt Van Buren's popularity. Then, in May 1838, he forced more than 15,000 Cherokee Indians from their lands in the Southeast. Without proper food and supplies, 4,000 of these Indians died marching west to Oklahoma on what came to be known as the Trail of Tears. Van Buren was also concerned over the balance of power in government between free and slave states.

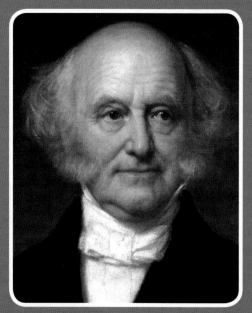

1841–1851   1841–1857   1848–1860   1849–1861   1850–1860   1860 AND BEYOND

Seeing the Light

In the late 1820s, a storm of religious energy swept across the United States. Many new religious movements developed. Among these, the Second Great Awakening stood out. This **revival** movement called on Christians to give up their sinning ways and to help others do the same. Its aim was to bring Americans back to their religious roots.

One of the most powerful leaders of this movement was a preacher named Charles G. Finney. The movement grew rapidly after Finney held a revival meeting in New York in 1826. By the end of 1830, Finney's nightly prayer meetings were filled to overflowing.

In the 1830s, the revival movement drew hundreds of thousands of followers throughout the nation. Its leaders preached that helping others would bring **salvation** to all. This idea helped further other reform movements, such as abolition and **temperance**.

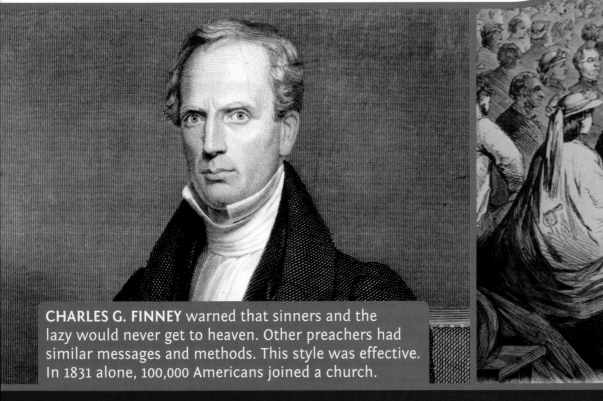

CHARLES G. FINNEY warned that sinners and the lazy would never get to heaven. Other preachers had similar messages and methods. This style was effective. In 1831 alone, 100,000 Americans joined a church.

The Role of Women

Women were a major force in the era of reform. Women brought advances in prison reform, in education, and in the care of the mentally ill. When the American Bible Society formed in 1816, female volunteers were its core. They worked to open religious colleges. They often served in educational roles as well.

Wealthy women donated money to religious groups. These efforts helped change society's view of the role of women. In time, women workers began receiving greater respect from the general public.

DURING THE SECOND Great Awakening, revival camp meetings lasted for days. Often held in tents, they attracted thousands, especially the young.

Movement Toward Abolition

By the 1830s, the abolition movement was on the rise. Many had come to view the practice of slavery as a sin. More Americans were demanding freedom for the enslaved and equal rights for all. Led by William Lloyd Garrison, the American Anti-Slavery Society started in 1833. Garrison had also been publishing his antislavery newspaper, *The Liberator*, since 1831. *The Liberator* called for direct action to end slavery. It suggested breaking away from slave states and forming an antislavery nation. Garrison wanted quick and extreme action to end slavery.

Another leading abolitionist, James Russell Howell, was more moderate. He felt "the world must be healed by degrees." Free African Americans and former slaves such as Frederick Douglass also worked for the abolitionist cause.

Also in the 1830s, violent mobs attacked and threatened many abolitionists. However, these dedicated reformers were not about to give up their goal of freedom for all.

IN THE FIRST issue of *The Liberator*, William Lloyd Garrison was clear about his strong antislavery stand. He wrote, "I will not retreat a single inch— AND I WILL BE HEARD."

1814–1815	1820s	1821–1840	1824–1841	1826–1830s	1831

1863

DRED SCOTT DECISION

Dred Scott was an enslaved African American from Missouri. When his owners moved to Illinois and later to the Wisconsin Territory, Scott went with them. This area was part of the free North. Scott sued for his freedom in 1857. He argued that because he lived in a free territory, he was no longer a slave. The U.S. Supreme Court decided 7–2 against Scott. The decision stated that no African American could claim U.S. citizenship. The person's background or home state made no difference.

Chief Justice Roger B. Taney, who wrote the decision, favored slavery. Southerners welcomed this new ruling. People in the North were outraged. The Dred Scott decision caused much public unrest and led to Abraham Lincoln being nominated for president. The first step to widespread abolition came in 1863. That year, President Lincoln's Emancipation Proclamation freed many, but not all, enslaved workers. Slavery was not abolished everywhere in the United States until 1865.

Reforming Society

Abolition was not the only growing concern. The Industrial Revolution gave rise to many new social problems. As people became aware of these problems, they formed movements of all kinds to address the issues. Voter reform had shown that changes in other areas were possible as well.

The temperance movement focused on alcohol abuse. Viewing alcohol as society's main evil, reformers made temperance a political issue. They also pushed for state-supported prisons. There, separated from the rest of society, criminals could serve time for their "sins."

Politicians and factory workers united to pass temperance laws. By the 1840s, temperance societies claimed more than 1 million members. In 1851, Maine became the first state to outlaw both the making and the selling of liquor.

TEMPERANCE PLEDGE

PLEDGE.

I promise by Divine assistance to abstain from the use of all Intoxicating Liquors as beverages

GOD is my STRENGTH AND POWER

TEMPERANCE WORKERS URGED people to sign pledges not to drink or spend their paychecks on alcohol.

1814–1815   1820s   1821–1840   1824–1841   1826–1830s   1831–1863

Helping the Mentally Ill

Dorothea Dix was a leading reformer in the mid-1800s. Her work led to major advances in the care of the mentally ill. In the 1840s, Dix began visiting prisons, poorhouses, and what were called "lunatic asylums." She was shocked at what she saw. Until that time, people believed the "insane" could not be helped. They were locked up in filthy buildings, often beaten and starved. Dix's detailed reports led to the opening of many state-run hospitals where the mentally ill began getting the help they needed.

DOROTHEA DIX'S WORK changed attitudes in the United States about mental illness. Her efforts in Europe greatlyhelped to improve conditions there as well.

A Higher Vision

By the mid-1800s, the U.S. economy had improved. Public education was spreading. Now, Americans began to set even higher ideals for society. The arts and literature blossomed as ways to improve the mind. This trend gave rise to other new movements. These movements were based on the beliefs that humans were basically good and that people could perfect themselves.

The Transcendentalist movement started in the 1820s but became well-known in the 1840s and 1850s. The Transcendentalists believed the ideal way of life was based on nature. From these ideas came **utopian** communities such as Brook Farm, set up in 1841. However, most of these communities were far from ideal and failed to survive.

Writers as well as good friends, Ralph Waldo Emerson and Henry David Thoreau were also leading Transcendentalists. Emerson heavily criticized slavery in his works. His thinking was also deeply influenced by works he edited and published in 1852.

Ralph Waldo Emerson

In *Civil Disobedience*, Thoreau called for nonviolent protest against unjust laws. Thoreau's classic book *Walden: A Search for Truth in Nature* was published in 1857. The author wrote it while living alone from 1845 through 1847 on Walden Pond in Massachusetts.

Henry David Thoreau

UTOPIAN COMMUNITIES STARTED in rural New England in the 1800s. In Massachusetts, the Transcendentalists started Fruitlands and other farm communities as well as Brook Farm.

Women's Suffrage

With the United States growing up, women's rights came into the spotlight. **Suffrage** was one of the most important women's issues at this time.

The first major public demand for women's suffrage came in 1848. That year, a convention was organized in Seneca Falls, New York. The Seneca Falls convention was the first women's rights convention in U.S. history. About 300 people came for two days of discussions and debate. At the end of the event, 68 women and 32 men signed a document they called a Declaration of Sentiments.

This declaration was closely modeled on the Declaration of Independence. In 12 resolutions, it stated that all men and women had equal rights. It was not an official document. However, it led to further conventions.

In 1850, the first National Women's Rights Convention took place in Worcester, Massachusetts. Nearly 1,000 people attended. Annual national conventions continued until 1860. Slowly, opinions began to change about women's rights.

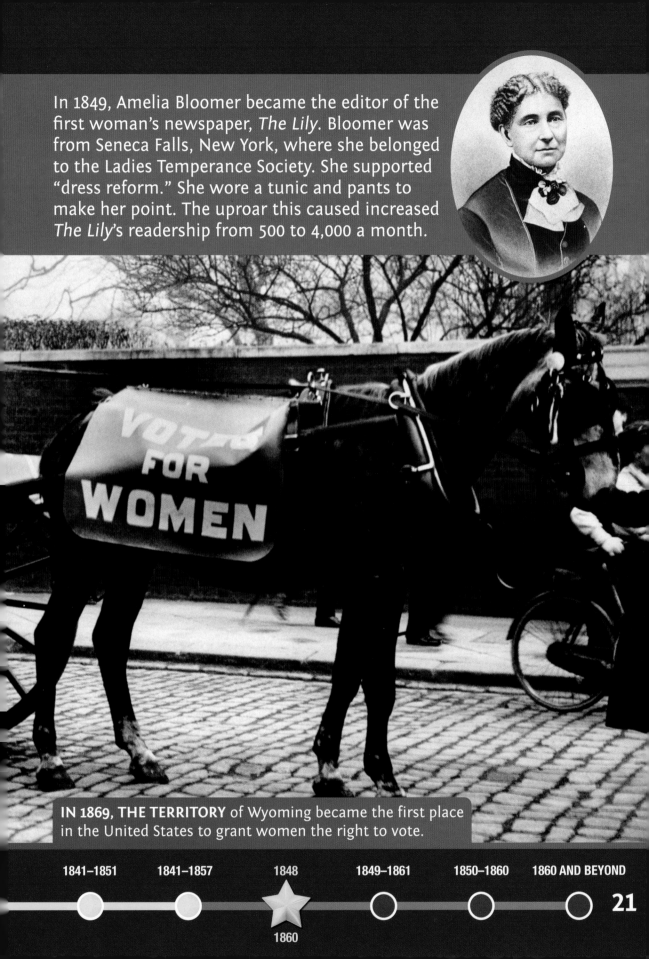

In 1849, Amelia Bloomer became the editor of the first woman's newspaper, *The Lily*. Bloomer was from Seneca Falls, New York, where she belonged to the Ladies Temperance Society. She supported "dress reform." She wore a tunic and pants to make her point. The uproar this caused increased *The Lily*'s readership from 500 to 4,000 a month.

IN 1869, THE TERRITORY of Wyoming became the first place in the United States to grant women the right to vote.

Nation in Turmoil

As the 1800s wore on, the issue of slavery became ever more serious in U.S. politics. Something had to be done to stop the growing divide between free states and slave states. In 1850, Congress passed five bills, hoping to ease tensions. However, the Compromise of 1850 failed. The good will between North and South continued to dissolve.

In 1854, Senator Stephen A. Douglas introduced a bill designed to create the states of Kansas and Nebraska. The Kansas-Nebraska Act stated that those who moved to these territories would vote on whether they would be free or slave states. People in the free states opposed the bill. They rightly saw it as conflicting with the **Missouri Compromise** of 1820. They also believed that if the bill passed, abolition would be almost impossible to achieve.

The Kansas-Nebraska Act passed. Feeling compromise was impossible, Northerners organized an antislavery political group called the People's Party. This party eventually became known as the Republican Party.

ZACHARY TAYLOR (IN OFFICE 1849–1850)

Zachary Taylor was the twelfth U.S. president and war hero of the War of 1812. Taylor was chosen as the **Whig Party** presidential candidate though he knew little about politics. He had never even voted in an election.

Taylor's presidency focused on the question of states' rights. When the southern states threatened to secede, Taylor promised severe punishment. The conflict was still unresolved when Taylor suddenly fell ill and died at age 65.

MILLARD FILLMORE (IN OFFICE 1850–1853)

Millard Fillmore was the thirteenth U.S. president. Also a Whig Party member, Vice President Fillmore became president when Taylor died. Fillmore also faced the issue of slavery. When California wanted to become a state, Senator Henry Clay created the Compromise of 1850. In this agreement, California would become a free state. In return, slaves caught escaping to the North would, by law, be returned to their owners. Taylor had opposed this compromise. Fillmore saw it as a way to ease tensions between North and South. After losing his party's nomination in the next election, Fillmore ran again for president in 1856 but lost to the Republicans.

JAMES BUCHANAN
(IN OFFICE 1857–1861)

James Buchanan was the fifteenth U.S. president. In 1856, Buchanan won the Democratic nomination and was elected president. In office, Buchanan did not take a firm stand on slavery. He believed each state should decide for itself how to handle slavery. In 1860, South Carolina voted to secede from the Union. Buchanan did nothing to stop this move. He spent four difficult months trying to hold the nation together before the newly elected Abraham Lincoln took office in March 1861.

The Call for Freedom

Since the beginning of the 1800s, Americans had come together on many new reforms. Abolition was not one of them. By 1850, the United States was far from united on this matter. The political struggle over slavery was not going away.

For the most part, southern slaveholders were firmly in charge of politics in their states. They were often able to control federal affairs as well. However, the population was exploding in the industrialized North. With more voting power, Northerners began to take the upper hand. This was dramatically proven when Abraham Lincoln was elected in 1860. It was a bitter shock for the South. There, ten states had not even included Lincoln's name on the ballot.

Angry and resentful, South Carolina was the first to react. The state seceded on December 20, 1860. Soon after, six other southern states did the same. War over the issue of slavery was rapidly approaching.

BEFORE 1860, ONLY about 30 percent of all Southerners owned slaves, yet these slaveholders ran southern politics.

1814–1815	1820s	1821–1840	1824–1841	1826–1830s	1831–1863

The 1860 U.S. Census on Slavery

Total number of slaves in the Lower South: 2,312,352 (47 percent of total population)

Total number of slaves in the Upper South: 1,208,758 (29 percent of total population)

Total number of slaves in the Border States: 432,586 (13 percent of total population)

Almost one-third of all Southern families owned slaves. In Mississippi and South Carolina, almost half did.

Total number of slaveholders, including some free African Americans in Louisiana: 385,000

Of these, 88 percent held fewer than 20 slaves. Nearly 50 percent held fewer than five.

HE SOUTH'S BOOMING cotton industry caused many utherners to view slavery as a "positive good" rather an a "necessary evil," common terms of the time.

War on the Horizon

The 1800s era of reform was a time of tremendous change for a new nation. These changes helped make the United States what it is today. With the Industrial Revolution came a national focus on human values. Industrialization brought economic progress and advances in **technology**.

The reform era pushed Americans into the future. Reformers had made the public aware of the nation's social problems. The many positive changes reformers introduced made life easier. Everywhere, people were rethinking their views on religion, class, and morals, or the difference between right and wrong behavior. Their attitudes toward equal rights, education, and politics were also changing.

Yet the United States still had far to go. Many national issues remained unresolved, including women's suffrage and conflicts with the American Indians. The most pressing, however, was the issue of slavery. The push to bring about abolition would drive the nation to civil war.

That war between North and South erupted in 1861. It brought further, more violent change. The war would be long and bloody. It would threaten to divide the country permanently.

The Civil War signaled a turning point in America's history. At the war's end, the nation would unite again. Slavery would be outlawed. Nationwide abolition would prove the greatest reform of the century.

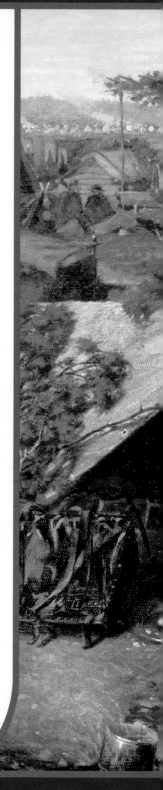

1814–1815   1820s   1821–1840   1824–1841   1826–1830s   1831–1863

SLAVERY WAS PROFITABLE, but the war over slavery was costly in every way. The South was home to only 30 percent of the nation's free population, but 60 percent of the nation's richest families lived there. This wealth did not prove to be an advantage in the Civil War, however. The North claimed victory in 1865.

Activity

Fill in the Blanks

Timelines are only a beginning. They provide an overview of the key events and important people that shaped history. Now, discover more about America's era of reform by researching in printed materials and on the internet.

Use a concept web to organize your ideas. Use the questions in the concept web to guide your research. When finished, use the completed web to help you write your report.

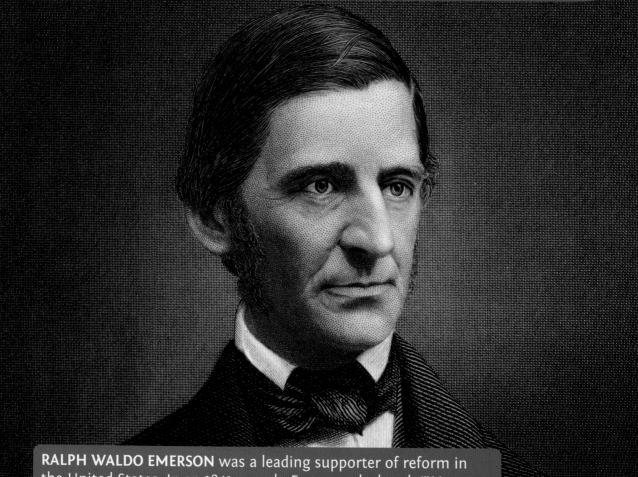

RALPH WALDO EMERSON was a leading supporter of reform in the United States. In an 1841 speech, Emerson declared, "We are to revise the whole of our social structure, the state, the school, religion, marriage, trade, science, and explore their foundations in our own nature . . . What is a man born for but to be a Reformer?"

Concept Web

Key People
- Discuss one or two main figures who had an impact on the times, event, or person you are researching.
- What negative or positive actions by people had a lasting effect on history?

Important Events
- What significant events shaped the times or the person you're writing about?
- Were there any major events that triggered some turning point in the life or the time you are writing about?

Historic Places
- Discuss some of the most important places related to the subject of your research.
- Are there some important places that are not well-known today?
- If so, what are they and why were they important at the time or to your subject?

Causes
- How was your subject affected by important historical moments of the time?
- Was there any chain of events to cause a particular outcome in the event, time, or the life you are researching?

Write a History Report

Obstacles
- What were some of the most difficult moments or events in the life of the person or in the historical timeline of the topic you are researching?
- Were there any particular people who greatly aided in the overcoming of obstacles?

Outcome and Lasting Effects
- What was the outcome of this chain of events?
- Was there a lasting effect on your subject?
- What is the importance of these "stepping stones" of history? How might the outcome have changed if things had happened differently?

Into the Future
- What lasting impact did your subject have on history?
- Is that person, time, or event well-known today?
- Have people's attitudes changed from back then until now about your subject?
- Do people think differently today about the subject than they did at the time the event happened or the person was alive?

Brain Teaser

1. Which president's policies resulted in the Trail of Tears?

2. What main issue led to the outbreak of the Civil War?

3. What was the name of a popular public school textbook from 1833?

4. Where and when was the first women's rights convention held?

5. To which movement did Ralph Waldo Emerson and Henry David Thoreau belong?

6. Who invented Morse Code?

7. Who led the Second Great Awakening movement?

8. What was *The Liberator*?

9. How did the Supreme Court judges vote in the Dred Scott decision?

10. Which president did nothing to stop South Carolina's secession from the Union?

11. What country did the United States fight in the War of 1812?

12. What groups fought alcohol abuse?

ANSWERS

1. Martin Van Buren
2. abolition of slavery
3. the McGuffey Reader
4. Seneca Falls, New York, in 1848
5. Transcendentalism
6. Samuel F. B. Morse
7. Charles G. Finney
8. an antislavery newspaper
9. 7–2 against Scott
10. James Buchanan
11. Great Britain
12. temperance societies

Key Words

abolition: the movement to abolish, or outlaw, slavery

civil rights: rights and basic freedoms belonging to every citizen

compromise: a deal in which both sides give up something

economy: the way a country's money and other resources are taken care of

federal: at the national level

ideals: ideas of perfection

immigrants: people who come to a new country from somewhere else

industrialization: the widespread development of industry

industry: the business of making goods and providing services

Jacksonian democracy: President Jackson's political movement to gain greater democracy for the common people

labor unions: groups of workers who organize to protect workers' rights and improve working conditions

Missouri Compromise: an 1820 agreement to regulate slavery in U.S. western territories

polls: voting places

Protestant: from a Christian religion whose founders broke away from the Catholic church in the 1500s

reform: change made for the better

revival: having to do with a reawakening of strong religious spirit

revolution: the overthrow of an old system for a new system

salvation: being saved from sin

seceding: breaking away or leaving

suffrage: the right to vote

technology: equipment or instruments made based on scientific knowledge

temperance: the practice of not drinking alcohol

Union: name for the United States, used mostly before and during the Civil War

utopian: having to do with a state of perfection

Whig Party: an 1800s political party whose candidates opposed Jacksonian democracy

Index

abolition 4, 12, 14, 15, 16, 22, 24, 26,
Adams, John Quincy 10
American Anti-Slavery Society 14

Bloomer, Amelia 21
Buchanan, James 23

Civil War 26, 27, 30
Compromise of 1850 22, 23

Dorothea Dix 17
Douglas, Stephen A. 22

Emerson, Ralph Waldo 19, 28, 30

Fillmore, Millard 23

Garrison, William Lloyd 14

Howell, James Russell 14

Industrial Revolution 6, 16, 26

Jackson, Andrew 8, 10, 11
Jacksonian democracy 8

Kansas-Nebraska Act 22

Lincoln, Abraham 15, 23, 24

Madison, James 5
Mann, Horace 8

McGuffey Reader 9, 30
Morse, Samuel F. B. 7, 30

Scott, Dred 15, 30
Second Great Awakening 12, 13, 30
Seneca Falls convention 20, 21, 30

Taylor, Zachary 22, 23
temperance 12, 16, 21, 30
Thoreau, Henry David 19, 30
Transcendentalists 18, 19

Van Buren, Martin 11, 30

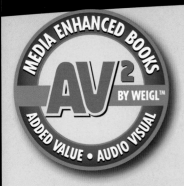

Log on to www.av2books.com

AV² by Weigl brings you media enhanced books that support active learning. Go to www.av2books.com, and enter the special code found on page 2 of this book. You will gain access to enriched and enhanced content that supplements and complements this book. Content includes video, audio, weblinks, quizzes, a slide show, and activities.

AV² Online Navigation

Audio
Listen to sections of the book read aloud.

Book Pages
AV² pages directly correspond to pages in the book.

Video
Watch informative video clips.

Key Words
Study vocabulary, and complete a matching word activity.

Embedded Weblinks
Gain additional information for research.

Try This!
Complete activities and hands-on experiments.

Quizzes
Test your knowledge.

Slide Show
View images and captions, and prepare a presentation.

AV² was built to bridge the gap between print and digital. We encourage you to tell us what you like and what you want to see in the future.

Sign up to be an AV² Ambassador at www.av2books.com/ambassador.

Due to the dynamic nature of the Internet, some of the URLs and activities provided as part of AV² by Weigl may have changed or ceased to exist. AV² by Weigl accepts no responsibility for any such changes. All media enhanced books are regularly monitored to update addresses and sites in a timely manner. Contact AV² by Weigl at 1-866-649-3445 or av2books@weigl.com with any questions, comments, or feedback.